THE ZENITH OF IMAGES

By

Jean-Philippe Guéant

THE ZENITH OF IMAGES

Cyberwit.net
4/2 B, L.I.G.
Govindpur Colony,
Allahabad-211004 (U.P.)
India

Tel: 91-532-2541153
E-mail: cyberwit@rediffmail.com
www.cyberwit.net

THE ZENITH OF IMAGES
Jean-Philippe Guéant

ISBN 81-8253-008-3
First Edition: May 2004
Rs. 150/-

Typeset by Vaishnavi Enterprises, Kamla Nagar, Allahabad
Printed in India at Astha Associates, D. N. Marg, Allahabad

ABOUT THE AUTHOR

Born on 6 of February, 1945, in Arras.
He starts academic studies (law, art history)
then devotes himself to painting, and poetry.

Jean-Philippe Guéant is the founder of the Transcendental Abstraction, or Transcendental Abstractism, his theoritical text is translated into languages

INTERNATIONAL EXHIBITIONS –

1968 –Lille Nouvelle Galerie d'art
–Roubaix Galerie Dujardin

1969 –Paris Salon des Réalitiés Nouvelles (Muséé Art Moderne de la ville de Paris)

1970 –Bondues Galerie Septentrion
–Les Baux de Provence Galerie Le Prince Noir
–Berne Galerie H.JUTZI
–Washington Galerie 21
–New York Byron Gallery
–Lille 'Nord 70' Muséé de Lille

1971 – Lille Atelier de la Monnaie

1972 à 1982 Voyages annuels en Orient dans les Monastères Bouddhiques

1973 –Lille Galerie J. STORME

1979 –Lille 'Les Uns par les Autres' Palais des Beaux-Arts di Lille

1985 –Le Touquet Galerie A.C.A.P (avec Soulages, Kijno, Pignon, Braque, Picasso, Metegari, Silvestri, Manessier...)

1986 –Paris 'Le Manifeste de l'Abstraction Transcendentale' paraît dans la Revue 'L' Autre Monde'-1986
–Le Touquet Galerie A.C.A.P.
–Stockholm ART FAIR
–Gand LINEART

1987 –Lille Galerie Règis Dorval (avec Hartung, Herbin, Poliakoff, Licata...)

1989 –Lille Galerie Sèlection

1996 –La Cote des Peintres AKOUN

1987 –Internet:
site Art Leader International,
site Galart,
site Poems from the planet Earth.

1998 –Hong-Kong HONG - KONG MAY (Hong-Kong Art Center)

1998 –Genève EUROP' ART 98 - Salon du Livre de Genève Who's Who in International Art Palais des Expositions de Genève (Palexpo)

1999 –Dictionnaire Benezit
– Venise Primavera a Venezia

2000 –Paris, Galerie Le Carrè d'Or

2001 –Buenos Aires Argentina Centre Culturel
–Revue 3e Millènaire
–Poetry Bunker, Biennale di Venizia
–Paris, Zème Rencontre Internationale du petit format

2002 –New York Artexpo
–Genève, Europ'art 2002 (catalogue page 169)

–Ferrara, Italia
–Washington, Nominated as poet of the year
–ARTE PADOVA, Italia

2003 –Stockholm, Art Book : Masters of Today, 100 Contemporary Artists,
–Orlando USA, Nominated as poet of the year
–New-York Artexpo
–Genève Europ'art (Katalog, Seite 148)

2004 –Genève, Europart 2004
–New-York Artexpo
–USA, Nominated as poet of the year
–Jean-Phillppee Guèant ècrit en plusieurs langues

En 1999 son oeuvre poètique (près de 1000 poèmes, à cette èpoque, sur I'Internet) fut proposèe à I'Assemblèe du prix Nobel pour la Littèrature.

(Jean-Phillppe Guèant thanks all the Culture actors and teachers who may propose his work to The Swedish Academy, Stockholm, while specifying his innovative contribution to Literature.)

*Certains de ses poèmes sont publiès dans quelques anthologies de poèsie aux Etats-Unis, et en Inde.

CONTENTS

FREE POETRY

I never was so
fond of metrical precision
if one excepts two or tree forking
verses
in ancient odds (& ends)

i did not sieve the needs
of angrily hungry readers
unless they appreciate
the freedom
of my rims

then i put them into mill
more than once it came
to be lacking
a foot at the end
of an haiku verse
i just add a dash
& , later on , slash

i used to drive
fork-lift trucks
for soul elevation till complete rest
& for crowning all
encore un sonnet de fait!
des sornettes

TICK TAPS

Time does not finish to end
to tickle
spins-les lombaires
& hours continue

pat & track

CHINESE ASTROLOGY

I, the night
the tiger stalks me
his eyes stare at me

but i am akin to the monkey
noone can shock or click me-nothing to win
i jump
from branches to sunday palms upon the trees canopy

from there i google
society clones
that surge

LOVE ON LEE

In the cup
of my hands-enfin réunies
i hold a huge
icicle
the iceberg of the world

the warmness of my blood
that passes through my heart
let it melt
& the ridge becomes round

love runs between
the fingers
& irrigates the word
love
is coiling up
so white swan happy to swim

but love can submerge-overwhelm
alas tokens are manifold

HEART GEOMETRY

From a pair of compasses
i put
the point
on the center
of a sheet of paper

i start to draw
with the lead
a large circle

a blue circle
now is almost closed
be quick! jump!
you can visualize
yourself
inside this circle-a round
of compassion

CHIP TO CHEEK

The page is bursting out blank
sparkling akin a
snow blanket

underwhere
are
in hiding

p
o
e
m
s

have a look ; view!-dare to pierce the secret
of the snowdrops
letters appear

p should be Pi

o is ô!

e is e-probable mail

m is aime!-aim of the sentiments

(transition)

s is whisling whilst making off through branches

poems murmur at our ears
the last winter winds

CHIP AWAKING

Musics of Lully
lull my sleep

the time is drawing
the curtain of dream

reveille!

i doze the waking
i still lie dormant

the scent of coffee
reminds me
savours from Orient

THE LAST TEMPTATION

The unconscious temptation
of our poor mankind
is the temptation
of a final big bang
as enlightenment

they have tried in Verdun
they tried in Nagasaki
tragical rehearsal
before the last dress one

ACID RAINS

Darkness is a
punishment on
the daylight

& if the sun then were not to
rise again
under all those clouds of dust
& vapors

& the winds
stopping short
how could our sails still wave
to escape the sea zymosis

(close to the poem action they are a-
pplying
fermentation in
industrial processes
& try to extract a new life
from zoeas)

TAO VIBRATION

In the hug
concept of uni(ted) verse
the words have drown
it but remains

now

one hurled silence
that beckons & eggs on
maple juice (a gift)

ART IN CRISIS

The text of her body
nonplussed my mind
ink scent
evapo*rates*
the sense

.com motion

EARTH LINKS

The earth
is proud
for growing trees
they are her children
she is very solicitous of
them
she strengthens
reinforces their roots which
compensate for weight

the earth became once engaged to the sun
(their parents had organized
the cosmic ceremony akin to
ancient tribes)
earth sends sun messages
through the trees branches
& birds born in the foliages
they are their links

more & more
acid rains or
nuclear vapors
prevent them from connecting

CATACLYSM

Spring
causes
every year
the same upheaval
scarlet camelias underline
emphasize
tu-lips that bloom
among the lemon fortysias
whilst white rhododendrons throw off sparks

tits
& sparrows c-
luck
winter kept green long
under its control
today Nature escapes from
the frostbite

inexorably

HELM AIM

Pebbles in suit pockets
to keep head
on shoulders
i offered daffodils
to her

she was a bunch
of mimosas + lilacs
petals of lips *en sus*-over & above

we put
grasses in our bags & poc-
kets
in order to seem "protected nature"
the birds in winter did not migrate
they landed onto
our feet
we gave them blades & twigs

the previous year
i had spent christmas
in a scarecrow jacket
birds had no color
i played with my life
i had no r*udder*

TRILOGY

From the box of thym surges
a poemshine
suns hinges
in angles que tiennent
des anges
-ants with wings

on the horizon line
letters gather to
compose hymns
throughbetween sea, sky & earth that
come to terms

pour verses on human kind
penn*ants* sail in the wind

ZEN HAIKU

gone sp-
arrow
is lost part of innocence

he-art*
whistling
at target

*heart

PHOENIX

From ashes
i rose-lotus

today
yet

i do not want
to play
fl-
esh petals
i acquired rules
precepts

headache
nymph-
s have
danced on my
cinders under e-yes of
Ganesh

before my rebirth

LES AMES

A soul is
however
will-o'-the-wisp
so *log* it has not
met
her soul mate

the second part of
oneself
we have seen before
come from ashland NE
& has worked one's way through the m-
ist forest of ages

o! so-
uls who meet again
you are the flickering amber
of my heart-
h

WITH OUT

A head
is not always neces-
sary

the best is
to sit
sometimes motionless
on a desert sh-
ore
on the exact center
of universe
& wait for not-
hing

while unseeing vague waves

DESTINY

Having a good
friend is-friandise
the best event you
can live
if it lasts
the sentiment may change into love

what a sweetcase

when you are a man
you are in the position to
become Maire de paris
if a girl
tennis champion

but
if you are Agassi
at Roland Garros place-Paris
do not ask Bill Clinton
for coming & see
c'est agaçant
on se retrouve grosjean

GHOST MIGHT

Strength of the
wind is
dwindling
we have reac-
hed
the summit of
slopehill-whitsun

this does not avoid
to climb on
whilst following
chamois spring-fawn color

TRANSIENT CLIP

Tortoise spectacles
on turquoise eyes
scent of jasmine came from her mouth

from her y
santal
she was the gypsy i got
in skin
her memory
doe(s) that my body still moves
& my thought is style dancing
dance!
flame & co

ça va passer

IT'S AEGIS

Il s'agit de la pluie
the rain of the night
-as Jupiter skin
cleaned (août) the
dust in
the street

the lane is zen

ho!rizon is o!-
pen we can pierce the secrets
beyond buildings &
buil-
ding

THE KNOT OF THE POEM

There is
a ce-
dar in compote
there are
sapphires on
the soil
et des grains de café
ready to get milled
further
an olive (tree)

with a lot of knots
all an alchemy

i wait for the denuement
yen in pocket

GREEN & FAWN

There
on the pond side
beside the ossify trunk
among the fallen leaves
that dried
a ween frog shows its back
green as a maiden growth
we are not in autumn
yet
a strong wind has let
twirl all the trees branches

doe looks at the scene

! TONE

Autumn always
alas lasts in
my heart akin
those violins
just before winter *-oh! un flocon
f-

lake
fawn colors of
fallen leaves that
spring in the wind

up to a blue shy
sky , irenic

* serait-ce déjà l'i vert?

WINNING THE CUP

She was a re-
al beach Venus-a mermaid
(scales sign-libre à vous!)
she uscd to wear
all kinds of swimsuits
she mixed the bras
she matched the bottoms

the set i pref-
erred-on the w*hole !*
twilight times
was co*bra*
in a light bahama breeze

what a fun at sunset-astronomical applications
art true body
belly button
clip-on
always spandex quality-i pero*rate*

ich redete in seiner Seele ,
Spiegel der Sterne-on line

NI AGARA , NOR ...

If i con-
sider this small brook
there
on the living table-it moves
-a plastic waterfall
destined to produce
negative ions-mountain air

after a while
of breathing
i stand on the side of
Ontario lack &
i try to walk on the wire
without any pole
aiming to cross Niagara-false

WHO KNOWS

We were so young
once and naked-so deprived
then the mirror* braked
it broke

or

we crossed through

it

who knows

(en tout cas
greyhounds and bichons were at our feet)

---

* Vanity by Hans Memling (1435-1484)

SKY RASHES

Lightning has
teared the
skies singularly-*sintax*
-beau coup de foudre en vérité
not the true light yet

one grey cloud has interr-
upted it (there isno
plural)

ECLIPSE ALCHEMY

The moon
was mirr-
orring
on the sea ,
sank suddenly
into
it
was snatched
by ocean
& bec-

ame a fish
array of sparkling scales
diving more &
more in the dusk of the mysteriou-
s waters

it reappeared sun , at dawn
sun
sere, blazing up
"dripping"* sea fire dr-

-ops

*pictural technic

ORCHESTRA

In the (fi)re
of si-
lence
i am copper-the brass
that boils
i brew

sfumato

i open
the window i
am a
wind instrument
that whistles the language
of birds

my soul is

1)the rain toccata
on roofs zinc , asphalt & pavement
which has just let the clouds
bursting out vapours

&)violins on meadow
blades of grass are
my bows-stringed!

>)dodecaphonic endless symphony
- fasol Mian(d)!

THE FIRST POEM

True poem
is al-
ways
first poem
(the fist one)
from The poet-yourself
at this very time
shed with the last rain

bouquet of verses
fresh-cut

genu(re)flect!-curtsey

HER GOLDEN HAIR

She was mine
of poems
when
we met
the mint of
her eyes refreshed
my mind

at summer

she brought watermelons
to sav*or*

l'or de ses cheveux
let swell
water* at the mouth-*etching
as a fait accompli

in the dew °
of her eyes
one could find
wee nuggets
° rosée > mist from rose!

ONE TIME MORE

Time
like a cycle
of poems
is always changing

glance only
remains

on old bikes

FALL IS

All is
very odd there
mist , gray , drives
us *towar*ds absurd
blind men show the way
to other blind fellows

fall is
inevitable

vade mecum!

shall we
fly like angels
beyond
emptyness
the body

of our text burns
parchments
are our wings

lors , nous fûmes
amarés

PAST

All the lifes
would not be
sufficient
to retrace
the path

AT HOME

Because of
the
w-hole of
the world
we do not
think even
of
autumn any more

autumn is too seasonal

leaves fall
colors change
sun is much less warm
frogs caw in
the smog

essential is elsewhere
fortunately we
should not
debouch into an atom season

ABOUT GOD

Religions are destroying
the concept of
God
they are driving humanity to
chaos

God possesses no real name

ATOMIC EYES

As i was just
looping
inthrough
the Empty
(with a magnifying glass)

nothing *particul*ar

my pupils > a n*atomy*
started to inflame

so,
what else did you want to k now!

POETRY

Poetry p-
lays hide-&-seek
under my
bed close to the clock

a-
larm

when the hour will be
rung
it will rush & tear
my soul to decipher it

but i use delaying tactics
i bowdlerize all chiming and jingling bowl
i Baudelairize
i try

REGRETS

Once in the
past back
i
threw
my
regrets away

as
egrets in the wind
they flew
from the pool
that mirrors
the surface of being

below (whilst)

among algae
thread their way
the koi carps
of thoughts

INDISCRETION

Des-
ire of writing
cast
my body off
the bed

early

power failure
no candle-all had burnt in the x-mas night

i set my self
in the garage
the plugs of the car headlights
were bright enough &
played on the concrete
wall screen

& i observed me
jerk the pencil

salad days

SHAVING

As i was
diving deeper & deeper
into the mirror-i use to shave every day

de près

i saw the ages of life
at a time
up to the prime cell

a sudden bright light
invested
my b*ody*

THE PATH OF (F) SENSES

If
you are sentient
on s'en tient

là

le sentier est
étroit

from_senses_to_consciousness

SEE SOON

Winter has just begun
but we!
are preparing the spring(ing) poem, already
that is plotting under the snows

(for summer: simmering s*ooo*n!)
-quite malapropos, i must agree

WHAT REALLY HAPPENED
(At The End Of Last July)

One happening

is something that may hap-
pen

keywords:
aquarius style
(with spout
(i.e. pouring lip for thee))
transcendental technique
white global vision-pleonasmos
transfiguration of a situation
in a given spot
it can also extend,
overflow,
fly off the handle,
reach political space

but

it must occur only
once

otherwise
this could not be called art
maudlin is not in season

VACUUM

Occidental is coincidental
a scene-le lieu de l'axiome
is always the west of an other place

as soon as one crosses the threshold of nth degree

CONSIDERATION FOR THE FUTURE

I am pl-
anting
for those who will
come after me

let us hope
that
i shall not
plant myself
in such a tall mood

while so plann-
in-
g

frisson! (cela frise le)

PAIN

From my wind-
ow i can hea-
r angels
playing harp

i do not
know how
to dry their t-
ears

a squirrel
colludes with me
hopping
between nuts
& strings wee vibrations
of the souls

collapse de temps!

THE SONG OF RAW LAND

C'est une chanson de gestation

the rainbow crusade

of the millennia

horn lesson
that lessens yet

the rescue of Future is not evident

but simply urgent
humanity homeland is in
highdanger

Icarus-*Icare*
who burned his own wings
was not diffident

thus

the sparrow can pass the gorge, narrow
like the hero arrow-à la Rose
ô! Rosenkavalier

ô! oiseaux du Manitoba

balbuzard butor fuligule

engoulevent

geai bleu

aurioles

SUMMER FLOWERING

Be-
tween the lines, shall we feel
the charms of the words

cauliflower
beets
artichoke

shall we hcar

wild orchids
from the lips of the maids & humid
nympheas songs-les nuits d'été
amid shoulder dandelions

shall we perceive
hya-
cints in the hairs
bis-
cuits in the eyes of the kids

and pierce the secret of tears for violet lemonade
or poppy syrup

shall we

discover

narcissi
in our mirrors

THE RIM OF THE TIME

I was doing some shopping
in the Hellemmes market "Leclerc"
(je fais la pub
encore cent ans après!)
i do not remember why i was there

perhaps for the rhyme

my attention was suddenly captured
by an orchids shelf
i chose one amid them,
in a lilac color,
on the plants department row
-no price la belle

this flower is pure beauty
& so whimsical-drinking hot water, only

to the point of a monomania

i drew
a new painting for background
musical camaieu
in my flat

rhyme

of the time wheel

civilizations are so fragile!

DELIGHT (ON A TRIAL BASIS)

A*scent*
a sensation

i stood at the entrance
of a flower

ô this poem
(what is the gender of a poem)
udder stopgap!
her eyes shimmer in the daylight

that brings art into the brain

NEW TON IN PHOTON

A beam
on a prism

no light transmitted
-see the extreme conditions
of this experiment:
the angle of incidence is greater
than the critical angle of the media

approach

a second prism towards
the hypotenuse of the first one

without (visibly) touching

will pick up the laser beam
though
there is no light between
both of the two prisms hypotenuses

(snom) the tunneling effect of the
photons is
a kind of Sixtine Chapel replica

factotum magnetism

secret of the creation
of life

true tone
peregrination

*eva*nescent waves

ACIDULÉ

Dear citizens
of the word

temerity!

do click on your tongues
we shall express
together as one
the sparkling buds
the butterflies
the rainbow lollipops

in order to escape
the deleterious
climates
that spoil our
atmosphere

BENEFICENCE

Daylight
is a delight
light day

fragile

i sip the blue from the sky
that hides there
behind the amassing clouds

MUNIFICENT

Soudain je
vis la lune au détour du chemin

un disque d'or
énorme tombant de brume
en brume
vertical
horizon
du vermeil
à
l'argent

et jusque dans la boue
du monde

mes pas soulevaient
un tapis de poussière
flottant entre les
feuilles démesurées des arbres millènaires

les enfants jetaient des pierres
au
"yaka"
blanc

après des jours
& des nuits de bus
& de char à boeufs
je vis enfin
le voyant aveugle
muni*
munificent
que j'étais venu trouver

*wise ascetic, in Sanskrit

FLORAISON GARDÉE

Spring is just late
this year
rains have stunned
the first blossoms

yet flourishing is kept

i observe gladly
budding viburni
& lilacs
a real delirium
bright white
pink violet ,
tender green of the wee leaves
-buddha pleasure, i mean
from the point of view of the creation

NATURAL PHEROMONES

Love of Nature (only)
is true aphrodisiac
-apyrous but apsis
were you walking
on the narrow paths
of our countries
herbs plants shrubberies
would tilt(-flickering red)
bent over you

animals would approach
& lick your hands
without any fear

and ,

back in town
for shopping ,
windows
lean over you
& wrap ,
encompass

you are packaged
thrilled?
(to bits or not et cetera-phénomène binaire)
fresh dead leaf was glued under your sole

ASK KEYS

Exquise!
she was planted in front
of my creation
painting on
canvas 12 feet high

ceruleum blue was lightening
on the curve of her eyes mirror
but not yet pouring
inthrough her heart

she seemed to be blind of feeling
however
seeds of wisdom
were rooting
inside her being
on pouvait discerner
dans ses yeux de minuscules abscences

PRECIOUS EXPRESSIONS

The favo*rite* time of the poets
is *spring*-one says
& , setting background , three other seasons wet
for gratitude

just after the Winter time
jumping from those ignoble torpors
poetry bursts out of snows
ice prisms ions-melted joys
frozen words
from the imminent past
hopping again , & hopping pong,
as racy express ions
claming light & delights

-cousu de fil blanc
le Printemps des Poètes

WAVES VAGUES

The poem is a
voyage
that drives
us through the vowels, so light, so flo-
wing fluid
and consonants, grave, so g-
rave
into the root of the Earth
deeply

within
the Verb vibration
waves of Silence

the poets vouch
for
immersing
inside the abyssal blue
and lost Atlantis, so vag(u)e

CONVERSANT

The previous argument was
really concrete
something bombous-du béton
it was not flabby
nor sticking
on eardrums like chewing-gum

if
i had bcen
a naturalist , a fisher
i would have preferred
words of waving algas
or carp bubbles
or the bamboo whistling-even plural
by neat proprieties

you will recognize me one day
i shall wear
a roses boutonnière
& wait for you on a fractal bench

pondering over
natant lotuses ,
natant on a virtual pond ,
& galvanized by foutain music-jingling chinking
pink blue green & jelly colored
as if i were in Mysore ,
suspended over the garden
in a myrtaceous air

Cupid! do not throw arrows
this is
a scarecrow
-ça ne fait pas mouche!
mais, fly!

AME* TANKA

As i went to the
market it was so raining
when i came back home
my sleeves were covered with
translucent pearls, chiming

*ame means rain in Japanese

BUDS ARE PLANNING SOMETHING

Des pensées planent
autour de moi
-pansies around my mind

i heard the bells
from the lilies
(of the valley)
yonder
is the wonder
on dit
in the evening primrose family

and butterflies
that brush shy petals:
the curtains of my winter studio

PLEASE ENTER A POEM NAME

As we walk in
such a nightmare-aux canards
we only step
on nettles fields-and tar

one cloud cries-c'est plus qu'allégorique
whilst dew forms
droplets
on brazil blue butterflies wings

roses thorns
torn our
hearts

all the *uni*verse
bows
under
the rain
God has no name !

DISPLAY POEM

Non que ce soit
un poème qui déplaise
ou dépayse

mais quel étalage
quel déploiement sur
l'écran-quel cran!
de visualisation
une mani-

festation de liberté

departure times
os tentation
far caterwaul

placate
assuage

SPRING

What is a birth
in f act

un saut
dans l'inconnu
a jump inthrough spring
a new cycle begins
old icicles have molted
into a silent pronunciamento

w-
heeled

round of sat elite
choice nurtured cells

brins de rimes de cerveau
gène éthique!

NET EVOLUTION

You are warring
& fairy tell
fears
people listen
half but
they hold their ears
cotton fields-hydrophile
come
over their mind
the day after tomorrow
they *shall* act
as it will be too late
time is chocolate
powder-all is rather crumbly